YOU ARE THE OCEAN

Love yourself, your life and forever be free

VANESSA SARATSOPOULOS

ISBN 978-1-7636119-0-0

You Are the Ocean

Have you ever considered that you are the ocean? At times quiet and calm, at others unable to relax. You are scintillating under the sun's love and warmth. Your shallow depths are the face, the surface, a front . . . though your true self runs deep. Deeper than you know. You will spend a lifetime discovering who you are, who you came here to be. You are made up of a patchwork of underwater worlds, of beauty and family, of fear and survival. Some parts of you will be discovered and others may forever remain a mystery. Just like the tides you will rise and fall daily. And through it all – this movement, this change – you will forever remain perfect. Perfect in your imperfect nature, perfect in the complexities and depths of everything that you are.

For James and Nico:

May you forever be guided by
your own innate wisdom and
know that you hold the key
to living the lives of your dreams.

Do you love yourself?

Do you realize that right now, in this moment, you are perfect and worthy of all that you desire? Or have you been caught up in the chaos of the world that has made you believe otherwise? If you don't realize this, then my wish is for you to journey to a place of true self-love. A journey to find love for yourself in the way you love your partner, child, friend, or anyone you can think of whom you love deeply.

I hope this book is the catalyst for your everlasting joy. May you see that life is beautiful and may you find the courage to step onto the path you were always meant to walk. If you are already on your way, may this be your inspiration to continue.

I arrived at this point because learning to love myself was and still is essential to my journey. I had a nice childhood growing up in Sydney, Australia, but becoming an adult and entering the world myself conditioned me to believe that I was not as great as I was born knowing I was. I know for sure that I am not alone in feeling this way.

I have worked in accounting, marketing, fashion, and retail. I even taught English in France at one point. In both my personal and professional life, I encountered experiences that chipped away at my soul and caused me to lose my way.

I became ashamed of my sensitivity and feminine energy. I was continually told and shown that these were 'weak' qualities. I felt that I needed to change who I was to be successful or feel happy. I made plenty of mistakes and failed many times along the way, and even tried my absolute best to hide those 'weaknesses;' but let me tell you, that didn't last very long . . .

After gaining more experience, and committing to self-reflection and growth, I now look back at my past self with so much love. I recognize now that my sensitivity and feminine energy are some of my greatest strengths. They are courageous qualities that I am proud to have. I take accountability for all my actions and also believe that the people whose words chipped away at my soul in the past intended to help me in their own way. I also recognize that I wouldn't be where I am today if I hadn't had those difficult experiences.

What I have learned is that there is a place for all of us in this world. Whether you are empathic towards others or riding your own waves of emotion, sensitive or thick-skinned, introverted, extroverted or a combination of all of these things, you are perfect. You are born with everything you need to be happy and successful. It is all already within you.

How to Read This Book

Feel free to read this book however you desire. You can read this classically from start to finish or be a maverick and read it backwards for a different kind of experience. You could even read it at random. My favorite way to read this book is to keep it by my side post morning meditation, then close my eyes and let the universe lead the way to one page for that day. I hold the book in my hands after feeling the expansion that meditation provides and say to myself, 'Universe, lead me to a page for the day and show me the way.' Then I run my fingers along the pages until I feel called to stop. Even if you don't have the time or desire to meditate, feel free to select a daily message at random; treat it like a horoscope of sorts. You will find that you are given the message you are meant to receive at the time you are meant to receive it.

That is the magic of the universe. That is divine timing. Trust that the universe is here to help you.

If you choose to read this book at all, know that I am honored. If you read this book from cover to cover, know that you will be taken on a journey which begins with recognizing that all emotions are valid. Then you will transition to a consideration of gratitude; focusing on what you have. From here, you will dive into intuition; connecting with your powerful inner wisdom. Then you will open yourself to love; for yourself, for others and for life. Next, you will explore the nature of time, so precious in its essence. Finally, these concepts will all culminate in growth.

This book is easy to read and intentionally filled with snippets of impactful wisdom. Though some messages may be brief, these are the ones that require the longest amount of reflection and can provide an impression that will last forever.

If you don't read the whole book, know that you were never destined to, only intended to find the words that you could personally connect with.

The power rests with you to find the right message when you need it most. And let me tell you that the power *always* rests with you. If you don't believe it already, I hope these pages shed light on just how incredible you are.

Finally, why the ocean?

In answer to your question, I ask another: have you ever felt the magical power of the ocean? I am sure that you have, in your own way. The ocean *never* ceases to amaze me. When I look at her, I feel an indescribable magic in my heart. When I dive into her depths, I feel a cleansing of sorts, a healing.

I feel free.

There is a connection that has led me to return to the ocean's edge for as long as I can remember. I have always found my greatest inspiration from the ocean, and I just can't seem to ever get enough.

As I was writing this book, I happened to listen to a podcast with the guest Robert Slovak. Robert is an international water scientist. His work—and the work of René Quinton, a French biologist commonly referred to as the 'father of Marine Therapy'—is truly fascinating, and I encourage you to investigate it further.

What struck me and has stuck with me is [Slovak/Quinton's assertion] that 'Cellular life evolved in the sea for 2.5 or more billion years . . . [and that when] life left the ocean about 400 million years ago, life took the ocean with it . . . [this] means that our fluid, the 60 to 70% of us that we call water is a copy of seawater'.[1]

. . . Boom! I couldn't pick my jaw up from the floor when I heard this, I immediately went to the internet to research further and drink up all the information I could in total awe. I thought 'is this the scientific, evidence-based justification for all my intuitive feelings, my love, my obsession? Is this the most intellectual and eloquent explanation for all the feelings I have inside?'

I thought that this information was indeed magical, and it completely blew me away. It made me think of the many times I've heard someone say that humans are mostly made up of water and reminds me of one of my most loved quotes:

> "We sweat and cry salt water, so we know that the ocean is really in our blood." – Teresia Teaiwa

Next time you cry, notice the saltiness of your tears as they trickle to your lips. And if they are not tears of joy, may the saltiness remind you that magic exists and bring you comfort.

Wishing you true, deep and everlasting joy, always and forever.

Xx Vanessa

1. Evarts Bosstick, L and Bosstick, M. (2023) The Skinny Confidential Him & Her Podcast, Tools & Tactics to Kickstart Your Health, Fitness, & Wellness in the New Year Ft. Robert Slovak Pt.2, 3 January 2023

YOU ARE THE OCEAN

EMOTIONS

If you are the ocean, waves are emotions. They come, crash, and disappear.

Some days they are even and small, on others they are wild and roar. Agitated by man or created by the ocean alone.

A lesson can be learned from the expertise of a surfer; one who rides the waves and feels them all. Choose and savor your bliss.

Know that you cannot attach to your emotions, nor should you let them define you as 'that' or 'this.'

Everything in moderation . . . except happiness.

I had come to believe that crying was weak through the conditioning of the world. I spent many years trying to hide my tears, though at times there was nowhere to go.

And out of my eyes the oceans would flow.

"Harden up", "you shouldn't cry here", "you feel the highest of highs and the lowest of lows"; the words of others became etched into my mind. The problem—though not a real problem—was . . . how could I act as someone else?

The incredible amounts of redirection were sometimes painful, sometimes a relief, and always utterly necessary. The universe continually returning me to where I was always meant to grow. I learned that crying is not weak, sensitivity is strength, and being vulnerable can be very powerful.

So do not be afraid to cry and share your tears with others. You will build connections, release draining emotions and be proud of what your vulnerability shows:

The ocean that is within you is also within me.

From this, together, we will flourish and grow.

Know that you cannot control external circumstances – the shifts, waves, and energies of others.

Know that you can protect your inner circumstances. Feed yourself with joy, care for your aura with love, shower your being with kindness.

Sometimes, the only way past is through.

She looked concerned, taking several deep breaths. Her father noticed and said, "Daughter, remove the element of stress as the task at hand will always be there. Take a break, step away and leave your worries behind. Then return to what you need to do."

She thought, *so simple but so profound* . . . "I can fill my time with stress, worry, and angst, or I can let it all go since my work will most definitely still be there regardless."

How do you know that you are the ocean? If you cry, notice the saltiness of your tears as they trickle to your lips. And if they are not tears of joy, may the saltiness comfort you and remind you that magic exists.

The ocean that is within you is within me.

Decompressing from emotions is so real and essential, whether they are your own or those you have picked up from others.

Imagine you have left a boat that has been out at sea, and you are still feeling the rocking and swaying motions of the waves. They remain with you afterward.

Take some time alone to release and shake off this sensation of restlessness. Meditate, sing, or dance to your favorite music. Rest, spend time in nature, do whatever it is that allows you to come back to your place of calm. Give yourself the gift of time and space to do so.

Something happens when I look into the ocean. The myriad shades of the blue expanse just do something to me. Something happens when I jump in. It is as if the movement of the water balances me and returns me to a place of calm. To my true essence.

I am home.

Just sit with it, that is all you have to do.

As you move through the day, take note of all the emotions that you experience. Keep asking yourself how you feel. Are you experiencing joy from your satisfying meal, anger because the bus ran late, surprise from bumping into a friend? Throughout your days you will experience many highs and lows. Recognize that these do not define you. A moment of anger doesn't make you a horrible person, nor does it define who you are. Know that this is purely part of the experience of life, nothing more, nothing less.

There is a strength in crying that may not be evident at first, especially because the world has made us believe that our tears are something to hide. Is it not the most exquisite thing to see another person shed tears of joy? It is time to make the world see that the brave wear their hearts on their sleeves, the warriors are not afraid to show their true selves, and the wise are comfortable enough in themselves to rise above the opinions of others.

Change the scenery.

It's incredible how the simple act of shifting environments can impact your emotions, perception, and state of mind.

You may sit in your jealousy, wallow in it and allow it to make you bitter, or you may see it as a gift. Be grateful that your feelings are indicating to you to change something. Jealousy is an emotion that can inspire you to move toward your desires, or to pause and be grateful for all that you have. Or both. Whichever way you choose to move forward, the magic happens when you turn and reflect inward.

GRATITUDE

A drop of gratitude into the ocean creates a ripple effect. One that impacts not only your own life, but also the lives of others.

Gratitude may only take a few seconds to express, but its effects can last forever.

Why do we berate our bodies? They do so much for us, every single moment we live.

For this reason, are they not worthy of awe and respect? Find what it is you are grateful for about your body. Focus on this and see your gratitude multiply.

We need to be grateful for the less than desirable experiences in our lives. The universe puts them in our path in order to redirect us to where we really need to go. To where we will be truly happy.

Don't feel completely disheartened by the job that you missed out on, the opportunity that didn't seize, the lover who chose someone else. Understand that these are mere parts of the ebb and flow of life. Don't discount your feelings, simply let yourself feel what you need to feel in that moment, then move on in a new direction.

Use this redirection as the motivation to make steps along a better path and trust that whatever happened has happened for a reason. At times you will understand that reason in the moment, but at other times you will not know until months or even years later. When understanding comes, it will be oh so bittersweet. Tinges of sadness may remain, or they may not, but they will not outshine your growth, nor will they take you to some place that you didn't need to visit.

Meditation has quite literally changed the trajectory of my days. Those that had been unfolding in unpleasant ways have been redirected after just a short break.

The power of taking time with yourself to stop and breathe, contemplate, repeat a mantra, close your eyes, or go for a walk can be transformative.

Try making space for yourself to step away from your troubles, if only for a minute or two.

Welcome doubt as a part of the journey along the road of following your dreams. It is the sign that you are taking a risk, pushing a boundary, and stepping into something new or unknown. If you don't question your choices or feel some level of discomfort, are you reaching high enough? If your life forever remained calm and continuous, you may not experience growth.

Welcome the doubt.

She said, "I am well, thank you my friend. I am over here enjoying the simple things in life".

She replied, "That is beautiful and inspiring. We all must learn to love the simple things, to find joy in the daily".

When the transient grand and beautiful things are gone and the awards and rewards have been claimed, it is the simple things that we have left.

Choose to focus your energy on those things that give your life joy and meaning, no matter how small.

I wonder how many other people in the world grew up disliking parts of themselves—their heritage, their personality traits, their home life, or the way their natural hair would fall—only to grow up to see that the things they disliked are the most beautiful pieces of themselves. To see that something they'd once wished to change is what makes them unique and special. To go from feeling self-loathing to being grateful for the parts of their identity that make them unique. The parts of themselves that helped them learn empathy and respect. The parts of themselves that others connect with on a deep level. The parts of themselves that they are now proud of that have shaped them into adults who are wonderful.

The magic of travel lies in the development of the mind, energy and soul. The expansion that the experience provides... the insight into the way that others live, love and think, and how other societies operate. Seeing things from another's perspective, walking in someone else's shoes. This provides a rich access to an understanding that there are many ways to live and a plethora of paths to tread, and that no one way is better or worse than the others, each are simply different. This broadening of perspectives provides you with a renewed inspiration, optimism, and time for space and growth. Travel, what a blessing, what a wonderful way to live.

He said to her, "Meditation is your medication."

She agreed.

There is no such thing as a bad meditation session, a bad workout, a bad time taken for your wellness and health. You will always be better off after taking time for yourself than if you never tried at all. Do your best and don't get caught up in worrying that you were distracted or didn't have as much energy as you'd like, or that today's session wasn't as easy as yesterday's or the day before's. Sometimes the difficulty is telling when you need the effort the most. And it is likely that you are on the verge of a breakthrough and period of growth.

Is it that you have been left out? Not invited? Has the rain cancelled your plans? Or are you blessed to be on the path towards something greater? Something that your previous plans did not leave room for.

I hope that you will see this was meant for you, that it is an opportunity. You may look back at this moment from a point in the future with love and understand exactly why things transpired the way they have.

Instead of purchasing something new that you do not necessarily need, look to what you already own. Direct your loving energy towards the things you already have. There is an immense magic in the energy of gratitude, and you may even discover something incredible you have forgotten about. Lay out your favorite possessions and remember the effort it took to acquire them, how much you love them, and how grateful you are to own them. Be proud of yourself and view your belongings as proof of just how far you've come.

Often, we get lost in the world telling us we need more. Sometimes we need to stop, step back and see this may not be true at all.

I love mornings. They bring forth fresh energy, so much opportunity, and a clear chance to start again.

The smell of sunscreen takes us back to memories that feed our soul. To days when we roamed as free spirits exploring islands and taking the time to read the books we put aside for when we had the time. To hours spent dancing freely without a care and not remembering the day of the week.

What an exceptional gift it is to have this sense, these experiences, this life.

When I look at the ocean, I feel an indescribable magic in my heart. When I dive into the waves, there is a cleansing of sorts, a healing. I am free.

What does your ocean look like? Close your eyes and visualize it now. Is the weather warm or grey? Are there people around, or perhaps some boats, or are you alone? Do you take a dip, walk on the edge with the waves lapping at your feet, or are you nestled on the sand? How do you feel?

Transport yourself there. Breathe in and out. You've arrived.

Take note of those people you can let your hair down around; those are your people. The ones around whom you don't have to act like someone that you aren't. The ones you tell your whole story to, without leaving out parts. The ones who love without judgment, give you their presence and show you their heart. Those are your people.

Seeing the world differently is a gift. Just like being weird or feeling unlike the majority is a gift. Don't let anyone make you think otherwise. It isn't called 'a point of difference' for no reason. What makes you different makes you special, allows you to question, push boundaries and see opportunities that no one else can.

If you feel different, know that you are wonderful.

Were you not considered, or are you destined for something or someone more extraordinary?

A beautiful person once said to me, "Everyone needs a hater". Simple, brutal and incredibly uplifting, this sentiment has stuck with me forever.

Just think of the colossal energy required to make everyone love you; how exhausting that would be, and how boring the world would be. Attempting to be universally loved is impossible, unnecessary, and will not lead to your happiness. Strive to be respected, yes, but don't feel disheartened if you have not pleased someone. Work on pleasing yourself. That is the key.

How I lucked out and ended up here is beyond me. Is there anything more healing than the ocean, more loving than the sun, more peaceful than being at the edge of a place where you feel comfortable and grounded and are at the beginning of everything else?

There is an immense magic in letting go. Freedom comes from letting go of the bad. But what is not so obvious is the need to let go of the good as well. Name what you desire and set your intentions, and then . . .Let. Them. Go.

And just be. Exist in the moment, be grateful for what you have, and watch what you desire be attracted to you and your beautiful magnetic energy.

There is something quite special about the afternoon sun. Walking to the beach to find people dotted along the sand, still warmed by those late afternoon rays. As if you are looking through a filter, the scene is overlaid with a perfect, deep golden hue. It is warmth without bite, comfort without sweat, satisfaction without worry. One can hold on to the last part of each day's magnificence with a dip in the ocean and blissfully enter the evening in a state of total rest. A gift on earth.

The only way to clean is with music.

If you are avoiding a task, pop on your favorite playlist to get you through and sing and dance away. The power of music will allow you to become lost in the moment and make a mundane task enjoyable. You may even grow to look forward to this ritual. This small way to find gratitude in your every day and elevate your life.

What is it about water? The draw of the ocean, a river, or even a shower. We are attracted to it—to look at it, live near it, float on it and swim in it. Is it because we are made up so much of it? It can calm us and draw away pain. It can take our tumultuous emotions and wash them away.

She said to me, "I will try my best".

I replied, "There is nothing more that I could ask for than that, thank you, I am deeply grateful".

There is no better than your best, and while your best differs from moment to moment, be proud and satisfied knowing that you have given your everything and your life will unfold accordingly.

Give yourself an ocean challenge.

That is, go and connect with nature whenever you are able and experience awe. If you find a patch of grass or ground, take your shoes off and connect with the Earth. If you have a flower in your garden, take the time to marvel in its glory. Smell the sea as its fragrance is carried by the breeze, watch the trees as they dance in the wind, or look up at the clouds as they move on by. This small but powerful practice is good for the mind, body and soul.

Every time I feel like I've been swallowed by my problems, the world has a way of reminding me of my good fortune.

The direction of your thoughts has the power to influence your life. The choice of direction rests with you. It is in your power to change your focus, if necessary.

Focus on your blessings, rather than those things that you may label as your 'misfortunes.' Focus on the aspects of your life that make you great, unique, and one of a kind. Focus on the joys in your daily life. Focus on the things that you love the most. Focus on the people, places, and things that you admire.

And watch your blessings multiply.

INTUITION

There once was a boy.
Who trusted his gut.
And he lived happily ever after.
The end.

If it doesn't feel good, don't do it. If the advice does not resonate, don't take it. If something doesn't work for you, try something else. Trust your intuition, your inner knowing. Tune in, and peace out.

If you find that someone's advice was right long after you could have applied it, know that the timing wasn't. No one else could have experienced the steps along your journey as you have.

The message landed when it was supposed to.

I am inspired by risk taking, the ability to follow one's heart. It is something so many can only wish they could do. So many remain in comfort rather than joy, wishing for courage but ending up trapped by what they define as their mediocrity.

Trust your gut.

The best piece of advice you will ever receive.

When you live from a place of alignment, the universe will create opportunities that match your purpose, and remove obstacles from your path. At first your path may not look like what you pictured for yourself. You may have to let go of what you thought you wanted. But with time and trust in the process, you will arrive at a place which is greater than you ever imagined, and you will grow into a person like the ones you have loved and admired from afar.

You are the inspiration.

Sometimes, you just need to take your own advice.

Stop making major decisions with your mind. Listen to your body, all the answers are within. Your intuition, your gut, your emotions, your heart—there is where the real intelligence lies. Stop trying to justify matters of love and desire with the mind. Just trust that what you love and desire cannot and should not be explained. Just experienced.

If you know something is true in your heart, why allow the world to make you think otherwise?

There is a difference between chasing and acting. The latter follows consideration, if only a moment's worth. You can chase something and end up lost, or you can act from a place of alignment and discover the journey you were always meant to take.

I will never forget the wisdom my grandmother imparted to me when I first became a mother. She said:

"The mother knows best."

That's it. It was the answer to everything. In the depths of sleep deprivation, hormone fluctuations and an identity crisis, I at first didn't believe it. I felt like an amateur in a world I knew nothing about. Though as time passed and life settled, I realized the wisdom in her words and how applicable they were to all of life, whether you are a mother or not.

She was referring to intuition, an inner knowing. An understanding of what needs to be done without being able to explain why you understand. An intuition born from experience; an understanding of the world gathered as a result of a fleeting thought or feeling. If you quiet the noise around you, you will find that you better connect to your own wisdom within. Trust it.

Refuse to be told or believe that you can't. Use this as motivation to show that you can, most importantly to yourself. Make this your daily mantra.

If you believe that you can, you can most definitely. And when you do, you will see that you can take on the world.

Tell me we aren't all connected, that there isn't some greater power, that you aren't intuitive—yet when you think of someone and then they call you or you see a text from them pop up on your phone. This happens too often to too many to be labelled solely as a coincidence.

Quiet the internal chatter that distracts you and connect with your magic. It is there for you. Even if you don't try, you will experience synchronicities and strange or interesting moments that will have you marvel if only for a second. You can move on with your day afterwards if you wish, but if you choose to connect with your magic, there is no limit to what you can achieve.

Sometimes speaking problems into existence provides all the direction you need to solve them.

Get out of your head. Stop living in the stories about yourself you don't like. The toxic ones, or the ones that you start to believe and don't love yourself for or feel stuck with. The ones that create a sick or icky or sad feeling when they arise.

Get into your body or out into the world. Move past your mind and see that they are merely thoughts, nothing more. When you realize this, you will see that only you have the power to change or remove them. You will then know how to set yourself free.

The only opinion that ultimately matters in the pursuit of your dreams is your own.

Connect to your internal wisdom.

It can be as simple as asking yourself 'how does this experience feel in my body?'. You may feel sensations in your gut, a tingling in your spine, a whisper of an insight may pop randomly in your mind. It could be illogical thoughts that you cannot shake, or a draining of your energy that is suggesting you take a break.

More often than not your intuition will give you understanding before the logical and rational mind chimes in. Flow through your days and try not to ignore the signs—you will experience that you are indeed magic.

There once was a girl.
Who trusted her gut.
And she lived happily ever after.
The end.

He said to her, "I know that I am destined for something bigger, I can feel it inside, I have always felt this way".

She slowly nodded her head in agreement, with a buzzing energy building, knowing this exact feeling she had held inside for so many years. They both continued to live their lives, not necessarily unhappy but not aligned. They chased small slices of joy, quick wins, temporary states of bliss. They continued this way for many years, and after all the shopping, holidays and fleeting moments, the feeling remained as it always did.

That is, until she decided to ask the universe to show her the way . . .

The answering journey was a rollercoaster of sorts, uncomfortable at times, blissful at others. Managing the realities of life and the path of her dreams challenged her in unimaginable ways, but she never gave up.

She saw him many years later, and to her he said, "It's too late for me, I've gone too far". And her heart broke for him; however, she chose not to reply, because she knew that he was incredible and it was never too late, but nothing she could say in that moment could sway him, and it was only he who could save himself.

Go on, make waves.

If you are being true to yourself, your desires, your excitement, why not?

It is time to enter your era of being extraordinary.

LOVE

I love you for you.

Not the way society says you should be,

Not the way I sometimes say I wish you would be,

Not the way others hope you could be.

I love you for the way you were and are and will forever be.

To me.

You are beautiful, you are intelligent, you are enough. In fact, you are more than enough, you are magnificent.

Just as you are.

For you my friend, I wish I could bottle the sun so that when you feel down you can open your bottle up, step outside, and be hugged by its warmth.

The sun's bright rays would illuminate what you have and what you see ahead, and its warmth would envelop you in love. You would take all you need from its never-ending brightness: light, joy, energy and vitamins.

Do something for yourself every day that lights you up.

I believe in love at second sight in the case of all love, romantic or not. Love that is born from knowing what lies beyond what you initially see. Just like the ocean appears one way on the surface but is incredibly rich, complex and different underneath, all things have hidden depths.

It is the second or third or millionth meeting where you have a chance to discover someone else's story. An understanding that drives compassion, connection and a clarity that may not always be discovered at the first encounter.

Be your own inspiration.

What if adults felt the same level of excitement that babies do when they see themselves in the mirror? We are born as our highest selves, though the world may make you believe otherwise.

What if when we looked at our reflections, we saw joy, love, and excitement? I promise, they are there. If you can find them you will see that you raise your own energetic vibration, which in turn makes the world that bit more wonderful too.

Instead of getting caught up in the mess, continually giving your energy away, or focusing on things that bring you down or people that make you feel lesser, redirect that energy towards loving yourself. Take from out there and move it within, with gentle loving support, with kindness.

I dare you to write down at least 3 qualities about yourself that you love. Put it in a note, inside your diary, on your phone, your fridge, your social media page, wherever. Keep going if you can. Add more as they arise. Make sure that you remind yourself of them all the time. Embed them in your mind so they become part of your everyday actions and conversations. Add them to your arsenal so that if you experience negativity, resistance or someone trying to knock you down, you can counter them with self-love and remember just what it is that makes you as incredible as you are.

Your first thought may be that someone is being standoffish, ignoring you, or not quite present in your interactions. Be open, compassionate and try not to assume. They may be battling behind closed doors, working through something privately, or taking their time to go with the flow. Just be there, as this is the most important thing you can do.

Start practicing better listening by resisting the urge to speak and share your story. Of course, there are times where it is perfectly necessary, the beauty of learning is that you will come to find the perfect times to interject and add in. Listen actively rather than thinking of your next response. With practice and intent, you will come to enjoy the beautiful impact on your life and the lives of those you love.

Let's celebrate the desire to look one's best as an act of self-love. Let's embrace the impact on one's confidence, one's perception of their experiences, and the way one moves throughout their days when they feel beautiful, handsome, gorgeous. Can you think of a time when you have felt this impact?

More importantly let us not label this as vain, or judge others for their appearance and tie some sense of inferiority or merit to it. Let's be open-minded and understand that beauty is in the eye of the beholder, and that our eyes see beauty in a myriad of ways.

Most importantly, direct your loving energy towards yourself. Whether through feeling beautiful or something else completely, you are always worthy of happiness.

Even when the world is gloomy and grey, you are beautiful.

I turned around and looked at him. The warm sun shone on his face, creating a welcoming glow. He looked me in the eyes and smiled the most beautiful smile I have ever experienced. I felt that smile deep in my heart; is that even possible?

In that moment I knew that everything was going to be wonderful.

What are your daily pleasureable non-negotiables? Do you have any? If you don't, then now is the perfect time to show yourself some love. When you do what lights you up on the daily, your energy beams and bubbles and without even trying you will affect those around you in the most exquisite way. Your non-negotiables could be meditation, coffee, movement, sunshine, delicious food, speaking to or spending time with loved ones.

Commit to your joy.

My non-negotiables are:

1. ____________________

2. ____________________

3. ____________________

4. ____________________

5. ____________________

It took me many years to finally discover love. It was when I realized that love is giving without the expectation of receiving anything in return. And although I have heard that phrase before, it was not until I experienced what it was like to want to give without being repaid that it stuck. When the act of giving is complete and whole and uplifting in itself, you are left with a buzz, a joy, an unquestionable positive energy.

Protect your energy, preserve your joy, and keep your peace.

There is something in the way we feel after spending time with others. There are some who raise your energetic vibration. Note that feeling and know that this is correct for you. Conversely, when someone leaves you feeling drained, it may tell of the opposite. Tune in to your energy for the real insight into the people you surround yourself with. You may forget what was said, but you won't forget how you feel. All the wisdom and answers are within you.

All I crave is a strong hug and real, deep, and honest conversation. Your presence is the greatest gift.

My greatest love.
My greatest achievement.
My greatest challenge.
My greatest lesson.
My greatest teacher.
My greatest evolution into my highest self.

My son.

Why is it that you are so kind, compassionate and positive toward others though you are negative, critical and unkind to yourself?

It is time to be your best friend, it is time to change the narrative which you speak to yourself. When you feel able to just exist as you are, you will love yourself for all that you are. In that moment, you will set yourself free.

Do you really know what someone else is going through, what they are battling behind closed doors? You may think you know from what you see and hear but you could be making untrue assumptions. Have compassion for others; you may discover that the person you passed judgement on is just like you.

Your challenge is to love yourself today. Instead of seeking out every flaw when you look in the mirror, step back for a second and be your own best friend. Be the one who looks at you with love and awe, the one who finds all the things about you to compliment, the one who says, "I love you, everything is going to be amazing."

Repeat this every day, even if you don't believe it at first. Keep going until you do, until you start to feel the energy of love shift around you.

Say 'no' more.

This is one of the greatest acts of love you can show yourself. Because when you say 'no' to something you don't want, you make space for the things that you do. And though it is easier said than done, with practice, like any other skill, you will become better at it over time.

It says more about the person who chooses to share their hate than it does about the person they communicate it to.

You don't have to love or even like everyone, this is impossible, and would create a very boring world indeed. If a person chooses to use their energy and time to bring another person down, then it is telling that there is something to heal within themselves. They are better off directing their time and energy inward.

Remember this.

Find your flow state. Be totally absorbed in what you are doing to the point where you feel that it is effortless. When you reach the point of total emersion, everything else will melt away and you will forget about the outside world, if only for a moment. You may not even realize you are caught up in the flow until a time later on. The magic lives here.

Listening is a gift. To be listened to is a luxury. Though this shouldn't be the case.

While hearing is easy, listening is on a level all of its own. It feels different when someone has truly listened to you, acknowledged your thoughts, opinions, emotions, and embraced your life. It feels profound to be asked thoughtful and considered questions, to have someone take the time to step into your shoes and comfort you in your darkest times. Remember to not only engage to respond but to listen, learn, and watch. This makes all the difference. Truly listening to someone is a simple gift with an enormous and everlasting impact, something you can practice now.

Believe in your ideas and plans and be your own cheerleader in the same way you would be excited for your best friend. Don't you deserve the same championing that you would give others without hesitation?

You are born with worth; you don't have to earn it. You just have to find what you feel you have lost. It was always there and always will be. Search within.

Today, instead of worrying about someone that doesn't love you the way you want them to or has not invited you somewhere or returned your text or call, be grateful for someone who does. Make it your mission to let them know how grateful you are. Spread the love you have been given and watch the ripple effect take hold.

"Let me tell you something about treats, my son."

"Yes, mother?"

"You deserve a treat if you have been good, and you deserve a treat if you have had a rough time, and you deserve a treat because you are you."

"So, you always deserve a treat?"

"Exactly. You always deserve to show yourself love. Now the idea of a 'treat' is defined differently by everyone, and of course one should indulge within reason. But what is the point of our days if we do not fill them with joy, kindness and love, especially for ourselves?".

People will try to steal your peace. It may be because they believe they are helping you. It may be because they need an outlet to express that their own peace has been broken or stolen. You can hear, listen and empathize with them, but by no means should you take on their pain. Acknowledge that it is not yours and send them love, for it is purely a reflection of their own life experience.

There is nothing more magnetic than your authentic self. Nothing draws others to you more.

Trying to be something other than the magic that you are will always be met with resistance, sometimes immediate and at other times delayed. The universe will always return you to your authentic self. The return may not always be pleasant or linear, it may be filled with a mixture of joy and pain, but it remains inevitable as a journey that only you will take.

Be in your authenticity and don't tell others what you think they want to hear; don't try to hide what you label as your imperfections. If you quiet your mind, you will realize that the things you see as your flaws form the fabric of who you are, neither bad nor good, but authentic.

You are perfect as you are, as you always were and as you will forever be.

You were born with everything that you will ever need, it is all already within.

When you believe and understand this, you will set your soul free.

"I want people to fall in love with themselves."

"OK . . ."

"I mean truly, deeply. The way you love your best friend, your partner, your child, your mum; you know".

"Hmm . . . Do you love yourself?"

"Well, I work on it every day. Some days are better than others, but that's normal".

"Explain . . ."

"I'm not perfect, no one is, though I am better now at loving myself if I'm feeling low or have fallen away from my goals. I have compassion for myself if I have had an off day, I do not criticize myself to the point of tears. I feel through it, know it will pass, send myself love and move on. I wish more people could do the same for themselves."

They all said to her, "Wow, you look amazing, you're glowing, what are you doing?"

To which she replied with grace, "Thank you for your kindness. Meditation looks good on me, living in alignment with myself suits me, and truly loving myself has set me free".

TIME

The present is all there is and all that there ever will be.

Time is our most precious commodity and the greatest luxury in life. It is not worth wasting your time on mindless activities or with people who leave you feeling lost or low.

Once you truly value your time, you will start to use it in ways that will fill up your cup. You will find that you can do more with less, and you will inevitably vibrate higher.

He asked his wife, "How did it go today?"

She replied, "There were moments of bliss and moments of struggle, my brow was dripping sweat at one point, as I tried to hold it together, hoping that no one would notice. Other times were calm and joyful, and I was incredibly proud".

"Sounds like a lifetime in a day. And now look at you, you've made it. Each day will make you stronger. Some days will be harder than others, it isn't a linear process, so be kind to yourself. Keep going. I love you. I believe in you".

Just breathe, and don't focus on anything else but your breath.

It is mind expanding to reflect on time's effect on perception. The passage of time can provide you with a clarity that cannot always be reached in the present. Have you ever looked back on photos of yourself that depict you at a moment in time when you didn't like something about your image.

When you look back you will see that you were always beautiful.

There has never been a greater time to be alive than right now and there will never be a more 'perfect' time than the present. The world is truly your oyster.

Dive in.

A 26-year-old once said to me that they felt that time was running out for them. At the time I thought that they were crazy but also empathized, knowing I had felt the same at their age. They were surprised when I said that the 30s are incredible and we spoke of so many people killing it in their 30s, 40s, 50s, 60s, and beyond.

Time is NOT running out and it is never too late. As you age, you become wiser, care less, and live more. You become more comfortable in your skin, and you may even learn to love yourself.

When you truly love yourself, you unlock the best of life in you and the years left of your life aren't even a consideration.

Every day, you can choose again.

For a moment I forgot.

I forgot there was a past; I forgot to think about some future, silly worries; to agonize about whether I'd had enough nutrients and whether I should have just ordered a small coffee. Because in the present moment none of that shit matters.

The sun shone on our faces and the sea sparkled, the sound of the waves crashing was soothing. In those sounds and sights, I realized the gift of the present moment. When you stay in the present moment, you live. For me this happens when I look at the sea, dive into the waves, or when I meditate, snowboard, ride a scooter, laugh with my friends, or spend time with my family.

What are your present moments?

Chase them.

Life will always present challenges regardless of who you are or what you are doing. You may be travelling the world, rubbing shoulders with the famous, or dedicating your life to others—in every scenario there are obstacles. Moments of grief or negativity, times of self-doubt or questioning, and the question of whether the grass may be greener if something, anything, were different. If you consistently let your mind wander, you will miss out on the magic of what *is*. You will lose power of the present; and in life; the present is all that truly exists.

Jump in. Don't hesitate.

We say we have 'no time' but have we checked the screen time data on our devices? The ones that are attached to our bodies that become an extension of our realities. Take just some of the time you'd have spent in front of a screen and place it elsewhere. You could workout, meditate, spend time on building a business, clean, read or even write a book.

Is there anything more wonderful than playing your favorite music? Sing, dance or tap your fingers away. Transcend your thoughts, the past, and future anxieties and for a moment or two, be completely in the present, lost in nothing but your bliss. Go on, elevate away.

She said, "Sister, I said that I would never do this, but now I have. I proclaimed that it was just not me, not my style, not who I am. I am slightly embarrassed".

Her sister replied, "Sister, there is nothing to be ashamed of. It is OK to change your mind. In fact, I love it when I do something that I announced I would never do. It shows that I have stepped into the shoes of another and have seen love from their perspective. It is an example of how I am expanding and evolving over time. It is cool. Own the change and feel proud."

We wish time away then look back wishing we had more time.

Embrace the present.

It is OK to take your time to reply. Sometimes you may respond in an instant and other times you may take a week, a month or more.

An instant response may feel right for you, but if it doesn't, this is alright. We must respect that we all operate differently, have different looking days, travel different journeys, and have different energies. Sometimes we don't have the energy at all. None of these ways of existing is wrong.

The message lands when you are ready for it.

Spending time with yourself is a transformative gift. If you have to schedule it, then do so. The most important relationship you will ever have is the one you have with yourself. You must give yourself the love and attention you would give to others without question.

Children can be our greatest teachers in so many ways.

I previously believed I could only meditate and exercise in the morning until I became a parent. The need to evolve has challenged me to find pockets of time throughout the day to do the things I love.

I am forever grateful for learning that time is our most precious gift, and I will honor this wisdom for the rest of my life.

GROWTH

I've come to a point where I understand that life is meant to be hard. It is not meant to always be sunshine.

There is a place for the storm, the rain, grief, the hard times. The difficult phases enrich our appreciation of the easy ones. I am grateful because the low moments of our lives allow us to grow into our highest selves. There are always learnings and opportunities to feel and reflect. Most of the time you won't understand the reason for your suffering while you're enduring it, but I hope that when you look back on those times you will be able to see how far you've come and understand how proud of yourself you should be.

With growth comes grief. Leveling up usually follows a time of discomfort. If you are feeling out of sorts, know that it is essential for your next chapter. Sit with it and reflect. Then move with it and fly.

There isn't only one way.

One formula for life, one path, one lifestyle, one story. One way to eat, sleep or work. One way to parent, love or give. It doesn't exist.

The best way is your own. As long as you aren't hurting yourself or others, of course. It is also important to respect that others may do things differently. Why should we judge another's decisions, happiness and path if it doesn't affect our own?

Today is the first day of the rest of your life.

It all starts with a thought—but it doesn't end there. Choose your thoughts wisely, though know that not all thoughts are wise, and this is OK. Your thoughts do not define you. Define yourself, as you are the only person who holds the power to create your life and the things that bring you joy, love, a buzz. The things that get you out of bed in the morning and allow you to sleep peacefully during the night.

When the struggle is greater, so is the reward.

The energy of working hard for what you want is different from the energy of doing something that you don't like. It is important to distinguish between the two. One is worthwhile and the other is draining—though not in the 'collapse on the lounge, satisfied' kind of way. Rather it can have negative impacts on many areas of your life; including sleep, health, relationships and more.

We must remain realistic in the expectation of how much hard work should be present in our lives, but we must also remain honest with ourselves about what or who is worthy of our effort. That is something that we can only answer for ourselves.

There really are plenty more fish in the sea. More people to partner with, more friends to call, more places in which to make your home, and more opportunities to create the dreams that seemed to live only in your mind.

In the moment, you may label an experience as 'loss'. In time, however, you will realize that your experience was there to pave the way to your incredible. And sometimes your path may differ from what you had originally imagined. Remember that in this difference lies a special kind of magic, that if you are open to receiving it, it will light a fire within you.

Them: "What do you do for a living?"

Me: "I vibrate higher."

Your job is to lift your energetic vibration higher. Do this and you will magnetize what is truly meant for you and bring it into your life.

You will not evolve as a result of smooth sailing.

Even though that may sound sweet, it is when the winds are rough, and the ocean is testing that you are challenged to evolve.

Remember this if you are feeling challenged. Adjust your sails and know that you will make it through. In fact, it will make you greater.

The evolution into parent is a humbling experience, should you desire to follow that path. You may think you would never do certain things until you have a child and find that in the course of raising them you do them all. Your ability to feel compassion for others—such as your parents, other parents, those that would love to become parents and those that don't—will grow beyond what you ever thought you would be capable of. You will see that there is more than one way to live, that your identity will be challenged, and you will learn that you cannot always be in control. And you will see that regardless of your status you must go with the ebbs and flows of life. Such is the truth of any human experience at all.

Your challenges are specifically for you so that you grow into your highest self.

A beautiful friend once said to me, "I conquered a fear today, you would be so proud". I *was* proud, proud beyond imagining even before I knew what her fear had been, and full of admiration for her strength.

Have you ever sat on the other side of fear? What an empowered space to be in. Free of fear, you may feel that you are on top of the world, capable of anything—and in the space beyond fear, these things are true.

Is there a fear that you would like to conquer? Start small or go big, it really doesn't matter. Just experiment and you might be surprised where you'll end up.

"That's so easy, anyone could do it!"

"Are you talking about what you're theoretically capable of doing, or what you *are* doing right now? We can do anything we want to if we're willing to try, but only the people who take action are rewarded."

The worst thing that you can do is subject yourself to unnecessary judgement. Do not criticize yourself for falling away from your goals. Acknowledge that the departure from the path you had anticipated taking had a purpose and know that you have moved past those choices. In each and every present moment, you have the opportunity to choose again.

You can swim, or, you can sink. If you sink, you may end up with an entirely new perspective. You may see how another world works. You may find something no one else has discovered before. You may end up wiser. You may end up finding a different way, or the life of your dreams perhaps. You may see that what makes you truly happy is not what you originally thought you wanted, but rather the opposite.

Whatever happens, you will see that it isn't so bad to sink after all. What matters is that you try your best, because when you do, you will eventually end up at the place where you were always meant to go.

The universe supports you, always, whether you believe it or not. In good times or bad, you are supported. In moments of abundance or scarcity, you are supported. When you're feeling up or down, you are supported. Those that seek to justify their feelings, to find the answers that explain their assumptions, to search for 'truth' in what they know, will always be supported.

Therefore, the question begs to be asked: "Why not think, feel and strive for the things that you truly desire?"

Stop making unnecessary apologies.

When you become conscious of all the times you say 'sorry' in your day, you will notice that all you are doing is making yourself small and adding an undercurrent of negativity to your interactions. Of course, it is important to apologize when necessary though you may find it incredible that there are many instances in which you don't need to.

Don't apologize if you are sick, for being a parent when your children need you, for giving someone a 'delayed response'. Instead of leaping to apologize, try to put a positive spin on things by saying something like 'thank you for your patience', 'I appreciate your understanding', or 'thank you for accommodating my needs' and watch the energy become lighter around you. You have the power to positively influence your life, the world and people around you.

Have you ever hesitated at the ocean's edge? The longer you wait, the more your thoughts take over and the less likely you are to jump in.

You walk in up to your shins and think that maybe you can't do it, you have 'cold feet.'

Try to remember that on the other side of that hesitation is a plethora of gifts: a cleansed and healed body, a refreshed mind, a balancing of emotions.

Why wait any longer?

It takes a strong person to ask for help. One who understands that it is impossible to get through this life alone. One who is courageous in their vulnerability. To ask is to make progress, to make an incredible step toward growth.

Be strong and know that it is admirable to ask others for help.

There is a place for you and your special gifts. With 8 billion people in the world, there is space for all. If someone is taking a similar path to you, it doesn't mean that yours needs to halt. Even if your ideas are similar to another's, know that you will attract others like you, those with which your message lands. Don't give up on your dreams because you think they have been achieved before.

If you have failed, you are not a failure. You may have learned something new that will help you better seize your next opportunity. You may have been redirected towards something better than you could have asked for. You may have opened a path to greatness. If you have failed, you have gained new chances to move forward, you only need to see it this way.

Don't fight the rip current, in the ocean and in life. Go with it. If you fight too hard for too long you may exhaust yourself completely. Be patient, float, and know that the hectic pull will soon end. You will return to a place of calm, the ocean's edge, the shore, your core; home.

Rainbows are a reminder that although it may rain and storm, there will be a magic moment for reflection in the aftermath of the chaos. Just as thunder and lightning can give way to a canvas for an array of colors so beautiful it takes your breath away; struggle and hardship can lead to growth that will enrich your soul. Overcoming adversity will enhance your strength and beauty. Look to your past and you will see examples of how true this is.

She said to me, "It's just a season."

She was right.

So simply and so beautifully put. This part of your life is simply a season. If you are feeling low, know that the hard times will pass. But always remember that the good times will eventually end as well, so ensure that you embrace what comes, all of it.

Isn't it ironic that every time you travel out into the world, your inner self goes on a journey, without even trying. You return home a different person than you were when you first left—your perspective can totally shift.

It's as if traversing the land and oceans opens your networks within.

And from this process of change and progression you grow into your highest self. So, take the opportunity to travel. Whether you choose to go near or far, on foot or by plane, it really doesn't matter.

Open yourself to experience your levelling up.

The only assumption that you should make is the assumption that you know nothing.

Be a student of your everyday, even if you are a teacher or mentor. From a position of being receptive to learn you will always gain insight. You will find gifts of wisdom in advice from a friend or family member, lessons in the mistakes of your loved ones, and direction from stories, whether from real life or fiction. Remain curious and open and the world will unfold in front of you.

She asked, "How are you enjoying parent life?"

She responded, "It is by far the hardest thing I have ever done though it is the most grounding experience I have ever had. I have not experienced a love like the one I feel for my child—it is hard to find the words to embody the vastness of it all. Even though I am challenged in so many ways every day, I have grown into a person that I am so proud to be, and I love myself now more than I ever have before, and for that I am deeply grateful."

Do not inherit the beliefs of others if they serve to get in the way of your dreams. Advice may be given as an act of love, or it may not, and you can receive it with receptive ears and an open mind. Remember, however, that the only opinion that truly matters is your own, the only authority that exists to decide your actions is yours and the only one that can walk your journey, write your story, and receive your glory is you.

What truly matters is not what happens to you, but rather how you respond to it, what you learn from it, and how you use it to grow yourself and others around you.

Conforming is outdated. How beautiful is it that we live in a time where there are so many examples of people living for themselves, breaking away from the mold, honoring their own uniqueness? How lucky are we to be part of a generation that is open and accepting and understands that there are a plethora of ways to live?

This is your cue to honor yourself. Be who you were meant to be and choose your own path. Now go and set the world on fire.

When you meditate and then realize that you are the problem. It all starts and ends with you.

Even if someone has upset you, you have the choice to respond differently, perceive it another way.

You are empowered in knowing that you are not a victim of any experience, no matter the obstacle in your path.

You are motivated in knowing that you are so powerful, so strong, so wise, you only needed the space between the chaos of life to realize this.

Be proud of your mistakes as they provide you with a way forward. You can try to learn something many times without success but make a mistake and you'll remember the lesson forever. Even if you have to face failure a few times, know that the lesson will stick when it is destined to.

She asked, "Dad, how is the world a reflection of one's thoughts?"

He replied with love, "Well, my daughter, look at this man walking along the beach. He is by himself. Some may see him as lonely, while others may see that he is at peace. What you see when you look at him reflects the way you think about yourself."

Don't give up, because on the other side of struggle is revelation. Revelations create wisdom. And in wisdom you will find peace.

Your trauma cannot be discounted, no matter how small. Though there comes a point where we must accept the story we're a part of and realize that we are in fact accountable for our own lives.

It is up to us to make something of what we have been given. It is up to us to see the opportunities waiting for us. It is up to us to make the change.

When you love yourself, you don't judge yourself for all the emotions that you experience. When you love yourself, you will feel an immense amount of gratitude for all that you have. When you love yourself, you can trust your intuition above all else. When you love yourself, you can give love in abundance. When you love yourself, you can understand that time is the greatest gift you possess, and you can honor the present. When you love yourself, it is inevitable that you will experience growth—that is, you can become the person you were always meant to be.

Your highest self.

Acknowledgements

To my husband Jordan, the eternal yang to my yin. You balance me perfectly and I love you deeply. Thank you for your support and love; I do not know where I would be without you.

To my parents, Garry and Lynette, the original water and fire, a Piscean and a Leo who make it work so well. You never pushed me but allowed me the freedom to become the woman I am today. I'm grateful that you are both always there for me. Thank you for your endless love.

To my sons, who have made me love the person I have become and have catapulted me into becoming my highest self. It is an honor to be your mother.

To all my beautiful family and friends, thank you for everything, I hope that you notice yourselves in these pages. You are there for me and inspire me every day.

To my spiritual guides, Celestina, Liz and Aisling, thank you for the direction and guidance. To my meditation teacher, Coby;

a guiding light in this world, thank you for the gift of expansion you have brought into my life.

Finally, to my editor Amanda and designer Euan, thank you for elevating my work with your exceptional talent. I am so grateful that the universe connected me to you both.

Notes

Here is some space to jot down your notes, thoughts, affirmations, and manifestations. Choose to use these pages as you wish. Create your dream life right here and now. I believe in the power of writing things down or drawing them if that suits you better.

I will be handwriting my daily affirmations and manifestations in this space so that I can remember to repeat them every day along receiving my message from the universe to show me the way.

Enjoy, much love and power to you. Xx V.S.

Printed in Great Britain
by Amazon

57831096R00111